The Art of Practical Catholicism 2

A guide to implementing your faith in our modern world

The Art of Practical Catholicism 2

A guide to implementing your faith in our modern world

George Charle Manassa

© George Manassa 2023

All rights reserved. Except for quotations, no part of this book may be reproduced or transmitted in any form or by any means, electronic or mechanical, including photocopying, recording, uploading to the internet, or by any information storage and retrieval system, without written permission from the publisher.

Published by Parousia Media Pty Ltd
PO Box 59, Galston NSW 2159
+61 2 8776 8778
www.parousiamedia.com

Printed in Australia
ISBN: 978-1-922968-53-1

Quoted versions of Scripture and the Catechism:
Catechism of the Catholic Church, Copyright 2000 - Second Edition

The Holy Bible - Revised Standard Version, Ignatius Edition, Copyright 2006 - Second Catholic Edition

Nihil Obstat:
Very Rev Wim Hoekstra LSS
Imprimatur:
+ Most Rev Vincent Long Van Nguyen OFMConv DD STL
Date: 07/07/2023

This book is dedicated to:

His Holiness Pope Benedict XVI
One of the greatest theologians of our time.

Thank you for your writings and for your renewal of the liturgy, especially through the Motu Proprio: Summorum Pontificum.

and

His Eminence George Cardinal Pell AC
The greatest prelate in Australia's history thus far.

Thank you for strengthening the faith of Australia.

Contents

Foreword   11

Introduction   15

1. Conducting yourself ethically   18
2. The art of respect   20
3. Apostolate in the workplace   22
4. Having a work-life balance   24
5. Etiquette for your digital devices   26
6. Do charity and help your community   28
7. Retreat   30
8. Creating and balancing social media   32
9. Praying more for others   34
10. Professional prestige - why we work   36
11. Sanctifying your work   38
12. Fighting racism today   40

13. Faith and food	43
14. Bringing someone back to church	45
15. The art of humility	47
16. Don't become complacent	49
17. Don't become overzealous	51
18. Preparing for Lent	53
19. Setting and keeping your New Year's goals	56
20. Preparing for the month of All Souls	58
21. Preparing for Advent	60
22. Embracing liturgical feasts	62
23. Overcoming habitual sin	64
24. The art of mortification	67
25. How to start a lay apostolate	69
26. Prepare for the second coming	71
27. How to become a saint	73
28. Staying clear of demonic influence	76
29. Explore the Eastern Churches	79
30. Catholic political influence	81
31. Pick up your Bible	83
32. What is manhood?	85
33. A rite of passage to manhood	87
34. Rites and rituals to grow your faith	90
35. Overcome materialism and consumerism	92
36. Make sense of Church scandal today	94
37. Make sense of suffering	96
38. Build authentic friendships	98
39. Memento Mori	100
40. Do not despair!	102
Conclusion	104

The Ten Commandments	106
Prayer to St Michael the Archangel	107
Recommended reading	108
About *The Catholic Toolbox*	110
Partners	112
Notes and Practical Resolutions	114

Foreword

Deacon Harold Burke-Sivers

The statistics are sobering. In 2022, the Pew Research Center reported that the number of Christians (Catholics, Evangelical and Mainline Protestants) continues to decline sharply while the number of people who identify as 'unaffiliated' (the "nones") continues to rise[1]. We continually hear from Catholic teens and young adults that Mass is "boring". An increasing number of them eventually leave the Church because they do not see a nexus between the faith and their everyday lived experience.

Human beings desire relationship and community, and those who abandon their Catholic upbringing will often replace a Christian worldview with some aspect of moral relativism in search of 'purpose' and 'meaning' in their lives. Those who have fallen away, if they continue to practise any faith at all,

---

1   "The projections show Christians of all ages shrinking from 64% to between a little more than half (54%) and just above one-third (35%) of all Americans by 2070. Over that same period, "nones" would rise from the current 30% to somewhere between 34% and 52% of the U.S. population," (Pew Research Center, September 13, 2022, 'Modeling the Future of Religion in America').

may join liberal, non-denominational ecclesial communities. Some take what they consider to be the 'best' qualities of various religious traditions and create their own subjective religious expression. Others abandon religion altogether and subsequently tout the banner of atheism or agnosticism. Most, however, are simply apathetic about their faith, convincing themselves that "as long as I am a good person, I'll be okay," (whatever that means).

We live in a society that coddles and placates us and does not challenge us to think or live virtuously. As a result, we have developed a distorted sense of entitlement and worry more about conforming to cultural trends than the state of our souls. We are more comfortable engaging with technology than having personal interactions that broaden our array of social skills. We pierce and tattoo almost every part of our bodies because we do not know how to express ourselves through inspired words or creative ideas, or we simply seek to mask the pain that wells up deep in our hearts. In a nutshell, this post-Christendom generation does not know how to think, act, or pray.

This was not always the case. The Bible is replete with examples of men and women like Samuel, Esther, David, Solomon and the Blessed Virgin Mary who personally chose to fulfil God's will in their lives. Moreover, the saints – like Maria Goretti, Therese of Lisieux, Dominic Savio, Agnes of Rome and Pier Giorgio Frassati – whose heroic virtue and steadfast faith assured them a place in heaven, illustrate the valuable contributions of Catholics who embodied the faith handed down to them. When we, like them, make the transition from knowing about God to truly knowing God, we will see more active and engaged disciples of Christ who strive to emulate their biblical and saintly peers, rather than anaemic cultural icons whose lives and influence 'fade like a passing shadow'.

This is a cause for great hope! In the midst of the present-day cultural milieu there is a vibrant dynamism and fervent enthusiasm among Catholics who fully embrace the faith without apology, and who want to know God intimately and personally. Among such Spirit-filled Catholics who remind us of our boundless potential in Christ, George Manassa most certainly stands out.

The book you are about to read is a testimony to how the power of God's love can work in Catholics who freely cooperate with the grace of the sacraments. The author's eloquent reflections and down-to-earth insights on living the Catholic faith are incredibly beautiful and deeply profound. Modernity's acceptance of 'woke' ideology, which has flourished alongside the 'cancelling' of Christian morality and the 'deplatforming' of traditional values, is hastening the death of objective truth. In the current climate, it is easy for us to get intellectually deceived and spiritually lost. *The Art of Practical Catholicism 2* is both an antidote for relativism and a spiritual GPS that keeps us on course to our true home – eternal life with God forever in heaven.

In a confused and hurting world where 'I think' has been replaced with 'I feel' – whose followers worship the trinity of 'me, myself and I' – George Manassa reminds us of the fundamental principles of truth, goodness, and beauty rooted in Jesus Christ and the Catholic Church; truths that intricately connect the mind and the heart to every aspect of our lives: work, recreation, prayer, liturgy, social media and so much more. *The Art of Practical Catholicism 2* is a light in the darkness for those searching for more than what this world offers, and a veritable feast for those hungering and thirsting for the Truth that sets them free. This book will undoubtedly draw many readers to rediscover a life-giving relationship with the Lord.

My prayer is that *The Art of Practical Catholicism 2* will encourage all Catholics to embrace the faith with greater desire, conviction, and fidelity. As you begin to incorporate these practical ways of living Catholicism into your everyday life, my hope is that you will drink deeply from the wellspring of God's infinite mercy and fall more passionately in love with Jesus, making Him the heart and centre of your life.

Deacon Harold Burke-Sivers M.T.S.
Author, *Behold the Man: A Catholic Vision of Male Spirituality*

Introduction

'*Lex orandi, lex credendi, lex vivendi*' is a Latin phrase that means 'The law of prayer is the law of belief is the law of life'. It suggests that the way we pray shapes our beliefs and hence our actions. This principle is closely tied to the Mass and the role it plays in shaping our faith. The reason I mention this is because this has a very important role when I refer to the title of this series as *The Art of Practical Catholicism*, and in this edition to begin by reminding the reader that the Mass is the source and summit of our entire spiritual life and that we can only carry out our mission in everyday life by truly participating in this reality properly.

What is the Art of Practical Catholicism?

I believe it is a mindset or philosophy which should be adopted by all the faithful. By this I refer to the practical mindset which is applied to the faith. That is, to take any aspect of our faith, and to then proceed to study and digest it personally, so that one can mechanically proceed to translating it into a practical strategy or tools, as I refer to them. So, the end goal is to find practical tools to take action with our faith, for the ultimate goal of growing in sanctity for the rest of our lives, and eventually attaining the kingdom of heaven.

The rituals and symbols used in the Mass are meant to be a tangible expression of the Church's beliefs and teachings. In this way, the Mass is a visual and sensory representation of our faith. The theology of the Mass is closely tied to the teachings of the Church, such as the sacrifice of Jesus on the cross and the presence of Jesus in the Eucharist. These teachings are not just concepts but are meant to be lived out in the Mass through the use of symbols and rituals. The focus is on the liturgical action and the symbolism of the Mass. The use of Latin, for example, helps to maintain a sense of reverence and mystery in the Mass, which some believe is important in maintaining a proper understanding of the Mass as a sacrifice.

The importance of the theology of the Mass being practically demonstrated within the rituals of the Mass cannot be overstated. The Mass is not just a ceremony, but a true encounter with Jesus and an expression of our faith. By participating in the Mass and participating in the rituals and symbols, we are not just passively observing, but actively participating in our faith. Likewise, we must not passively study our faith, but implement it in our lives, drawing our strength from the liturgy.

In this edition of *The Art of Practical Catholicism* I will equip you with the tools to take action for our time, with many different aspects of the faith and human virtue addressed. As always, I do not impose my own practical tools on you, rather, I leave room for note-taking at the back of the book, so as to encourage your active participation. Some of these topics are based upon my own personal reflections and practical tools generated when preparing for each episode of

The Catholic Toolbox radio show and others are simply ones which resonate with me personally.

I pray that the reader will study the faith through the rich theological tradition which has been passed down to us through the ages until today (*lex credendi*). Then to pray and participate in the Holy Sacrifice of the Mass with utmost devotion (*lex orandi*) and therefore take decisive action with their faith in our modern world today.

Chapter 1

Conducting yourself ethically

CONDUCTING oneself ethically in everyday life and living with integrity is essential for building a harmonious and just society. Ethics refers to the principles and values that govern our behaviour and decisions, while integrity refers to adhering to those values and being honest and transparent in our actions. In today's complex world, it can be challenging to maintain these principles, but with awareness, effort, and discipline, it is possible to live a life guided by ethics and integrity.

Here are three practical tools that you can use to help you take action and live with integrity:

1. Reflect on your values. The first step in conducting yourself ethically is to reflect on your values and beliefs. This involves understanding what is important to you and what you stand for. Ask yourself questions such as 'What are my personal values? What do I believe is right and wrong? What are my moral obligations to

others?' By understanding your values, you can use them as a guide to make ethical decisions.

2. Practise active listening. Another essential tool for ethical conduct is active listening. This means taking the time to listen to others and to understand their perspectives, even if you don't agree with them. Active listening is a key component of respectful communication and helps to build trust and mutual understanding. When you listen actively, you are more likely to identify ethical dilemmas and make decisions that are in line with your values.

3. Take responsibility for your actions. Finally, to live with integrity, you must take responsibility for your actions. This means being accountable for the decisions you make and the impact they have on others. When you make a mistake, acknowledge it, apologise, and take steps to make amends. By taking responsibility for your actions, you demonstrate that you are committed to ethical conduct and integrity.

Living a life guided by ethics and human virtue requires effort, discipline, and awareness. By reflecting on your values, practising active listening, and taking responsibility for your actions, you can make ethical decisions and live a life guided by integrity. Remember, the choices you make and the actions you take every day can have a lasting impact on others and the world around you.

Chapter 2

The art of respect

ONE important aspect of becoming a virtuous person is respecting others, and this is something that can be achieved both in your personal life as well as in your professional life. In the workplace, respecting others means recognising and valuing the contributions of your co-workers.

It means avoiding gossip and spreading rumours, and instead engaging in open and honest communication. It also means acknowledging and accepting the differences in people, including their backgrounds, beliefs, and perspectives. When it comes to your friends and family, respecting others means treating them with kindness and compassion.

It means listening to their opinions and thoughts, even if they differ from your own. It also means being honest and trustworthy, and being there for them when they need you. Here are three practical tools to help you take action, putting such human struggle into action within your day-to-day life:

1. Practise active empathy. Active empathy is something vital for the character growth of an individual. In order to take action, one technique would be to stop and ask how someone feels in each situation, to mentally visualise how they feel, and then to apply the golden rule of the Gospel to treat others as you ought to be treated (Matthew 7:12).

2. Be mindful of your words and actions. The manner in which you speak and carry yourself can have significant implications for evangelisation and interaction towards others. This includes how you come across to others, and if you make an effort to avoid actions that might be harmful or offensive. A common way in workplaces and in social settings is to avoid engaging in any form of gossip or defamatory remarks towards others, instead focusing on the positive aspects of people and situations.

3. Show gratitude. One easy but effective method to respect others is to express thanks. Let your employees, friends and family know how much you value their contributions by recognising them. Say "thank you" or write them a note to express how much you appreciate their efforts. By expressing thankfulness, you let the other person know that you respect and value them and are appreciative of their contribution to your life.

By using these tips, you can start treating people with respect in your daily interactions and start developing human virtue. Keep in mind that respect is a two-way street; the more respect you show others, the more likely it is that you will receive it in return.

Chapter 3

Apostolate in the workplace

I FIRMLY think that it is my obligation to aid in others' spiritual ascent. The principles of St Josemaría Escrivá – a Spanish priest and the founder of the global Catholic lay group Opus Dei – have been very pivotal in our modern world of this conviction. Any labour can be made sacred, and it can be an occasion to practise apostolate, that is, to proclaim the Good News and bring others to Christ, according to St Josemaría. There are various useful instruments that you can utilise to conduct apostolate at work and bring many souls closer to Our Lord.

Prayer comes first. The cornerstone of any apostolate is prayer, which supports any missionary concentration and a spiritual perspective. You may strengthen your relationship with God and obtain the grace and direction you need to effectively help others find God in your everyday dealings.

1. One practical way that you can do this is by sharing your faith with co-workers. This might involve inviting them

to join you for a spiritual activity or sharing with them books or other resources that have been meaningful in your own spiritual journey. Participating in workplace opportunities for professional development can be a means to eventually mention your faith in conversation, as growing in human virtue can better dispose people around us to receive divine truth.

2. Another practical way that you can do apostolate is by volunteering in your community. This can include volunteering at a local soup kitchen or local charity.

3. Finally, support other Catholics in their own faith journeys by offering words of encouragement, prayer and support. This might involve mentoring someone or simply being a listening ear and a source of support to someone who is struggling.

You owe it to others to aid their spiritual ascent. Every job can be made sacred and can be a chance for apostolate, according to St Josemaría Escrivá. Start by growing in your own personal holiness, and then you will be able to allow this to overflow like a fountain to others and help them grow closer to God.

Chapter 4

Having a work-life balance

YOU try to live a life that is focused on God as a Catholic. This includes juggling your job and personal obligations in a way that respects your beliefs and core principles. It can be difficult to strike a balance between work and life that is God-centred, but with a little work and the correct resources, it is possible.

It's crucial to keep in mind that everything you do, whether at work or at home, should revolve around God. Putting Him first in your thoughts, deeds and decisions entails doing just that. It's simpler to stay grounded and make decisions that are consistent with your values when you begin each day with a focus on God.

Here are three practical tools you can use to help you to keep in God's presence while carrying out your busy daily life:

1. Spend time each day for prayer and devotions so that you can communicate with God. This can be as easy

as spending a few minutes each morning in solitude or partaking in a daily devotional like the Rosary.

2. Managing your time effectively is paramount. Diarise your time and assign events, tasks or projects a priority based on what is most essential to you. Make time for spiritually nourishing pursuits like volunteer work and family time and try to compartmentalise social media into times where you may not be engaging with your family outside work hours, like travelling on a train or while waiting for an appointment.

3. Last, but not least, don't be scared to ask for help from others. This can involve finding a spiritual mentor, integrating into a faith group, or asking friends and family for help. Having a support network consisting of people you trust around you will solidify your growth and help you to stay focused.

You can become closer to a God-centred work-life balance by implementing these useful tools into your everyday life. Be patient with yourself and have faith in God's plan, since the path to a balanced existence is a lifelong one. Maintain your spiritual focus, give priority to what matters most and ask for help when you require it. You may lead a life that is focused on God, one that is full of purpose and peace, with time and effort.

Chapter 5

Etiquette for your digital devices

SOCIAL media can only be accessed through a digital device. A wide range of digital gadgets are available and are being developed even as you read this! These could be desktop or laptop computers, smartphones, or both, and who knows what will be available in the next 10 years or less!

It's crucial to understand how to use your digital gadgets if you want to succeed in today's society. One reason why people need to know how to use a device is in case of an emergency. People need to know how much of their device they should use each day in addition to how it functions. Too much time spent in front of a computer screen has led to habitual problems and health issues in different areas for people, and behind this is the imbalance and disproportionate use of digital devices.

You can master your day by maintaining balance in how you use your digital devices. You may recapture the time spent on your phone, quantify it and redirect those hours to better use.

1. Don't use your phone while eating with others. When someone is using their phone while eating, almost everyone notices. You should focus on the present when you're eating with friends and family. Although tempting while waiting for your Chinese food or after your plate has been taken away, it is imperative to respect those with whom you are dining. Because it forces people to be close to one another, this moment is unique. There is a close connection between communion with others and dining with them, and this time should be optimised to improve relationships with anyone who we are sharing a meal with. For the exception of emergency calls or messages, there will be plenty of time later to look at your gadget. In conclusion, no one at the table should use their phone until the meal is over, whatever that may mean in differing cultures or circumstances.

2. Limit your phone use in conversations with others. This is another golden rule outside the meal situations, to show that you value others, especially if we want to be ambassadors of the Gospel, for to do so, we need to value others and go deeper into conversation with them and understand their perspective. Minimising phone use and not prioritising phone use while with others, unless there are important messages or calls that you need to make, is very important to bringing value to the time you may spend with others.

Chapter 6

Do charity and help your community

There has always been a group of people who are less fortunate than the average individual throughout the course of human history. They might have mental impairments. Even someone with a well-paying job is susceptible to losing their livelihood and undergoing unfortunate struggles in life. They thereafter descend into poverty.

Giving of yourself to the larger good is a fantastic approach to carrying out the corporal works of mercy. It does not have to be complicated – all you have to do is lend a hand at local activities in order to aid the less fortunate.

Everyone who wants to start volunteering must look into the choices that are accessible in their community. A straightforward Google search is an excellent place to start. Find out where the local homeless kitchens and community ministries are located. There may be listings for local volunteer opportunities in your local newspaper. You can have access to outreach alternatives through your church.

1. Put out some effort to show up. Make an effort to show up and not be tempted to delay getting involved. Procrastination can be a serious obstacle in this area, because there is always something else of monetary or social benefit that can be done during this time, rather than helping those in the community free of charge.

2. Create a program for outreach. You may setup your own outreach program to aid the underprivileged if you feel up to the challenge, if you have your own niche or area which you wish to focus on. This may be an option initially depending on your skills or experience, or eventually as you gain experience through assisting an organisation.

3. Encourage friends and family to get involved as well. Making this a family-friendly activity or using this as a means of social activity with your friends can be a way to encourage people to get involved. Rather than asking for help during free time, this is a great way to rewire your marketing approach to others.

Chapter 7

Retreat

Even Our Lord needed a retreat on Mount Tabor, where he went up on a mountain and spent time apart from the world and reconnected with the Father. Time apart from the world by retreating away from the world, helps us to grow closer in friendship with God and then come back renewed. Every Catholic should make an annual retreat.

The purpose of a retreat is to physically unwind, pray, reflect and make resolutions for coming back to the world. Everyone requires a break from time to time. Here are some practical tools in preparing to make a retreat:

(NB. Speak your mind if you want to make sure no one messages you while you're on break. Inform your loved ones that you will be disconnecting for a set period of time, whether it is a couple of days or a week. You also won't want to think about working while on retreat.)

1. Find an organisation that offers a silent retreat only. Since the prime aim of your rest period is to recuperate spiritually and put yourself in a state of contemplation, it is imperative that you do this only in silence, where you can hear God clearly.

2. Reflect. Reflect on your current state in life and think about what changes need to happen in your life, through the program of reflection and spiritual exercises on the particular retreat you have chosen.

3. Practical resolutions. *The Catholic Toolbox* is all about taking action by identifying issues or areas which need improving, taking note of them and then finally creating a practical strategy to take action. What better way to do so than on a retreat, which is the very limited time you will ever have in one year to switch off from the world.

Remember, even Our Lord needed a retreat, on Mount Tabor!

Chapter 8

Creating and balancing social media

SOCIAL media is an effective instrument for influence and connection. There are so many businesses and websites dedicated to assisting authors in popularising their accounts.

Here are three practical tools that will assist you with selecting and balancing social media:

1. Understand the platform. You must be familiar with the platform's features and how they may support your goal of digitally engaging with people as you set out on your journey to increase your social media presence. Discern what social media platforms you really need and create profiles for those which you will actually make use of, in an effort to keep yourself decluttered from the often demanding online world.

2. Stop using social media. People often have a social media fast during Lent or other times to rejuvenate and focus on the real world and their spiritual life. One's

mental health may suffer as a result of concentrating on what other people are doing on social media.

3. Making sure that your daily usage doesn't go above an hour is an excellent way to gauge how much time you spend on social media. This gives you one hour to use social media, assuming you work from 9am to 5pm. This gives you many hours to spend on more fulfilling things. So don't forget to use the one-hour rule.

Chapter 9

Praying more for others

ONE'S spiritual life revolves around prayer, and it is crucial to pray for others as well as for oneself. It may have a significant influence on someone's life to pray for others as a means to demonstrate our love and care for those who are in need. Catholics can increase their prayers for others by using the following three useful strategies below:

1. The Rosary is a potent instrument to pray for other people, since the very nature of this prayer is asking Our Lady to pray for us. Perhaps as the nature of the prayer suggests, we will grow in a habit of interceding for others ourselves through her inspiration.

2. A novena is a series of prayers recited over the course of nine days. Taking up a novena will be a useful tool to assist friends or family who need our prayers. These prayers are frequently said in honour of a certain saint. Concentrating your prayer through a novena is an excellent way to grow in our love of others.

3. During the Holy Sacrifice of the Mass, you can unite your prayers for the needs of others. This can be done privately through your own prayers or publicly, by asking a priest to offer Mass for your intentions (there may be a donation required based on your local custom), and it is a powerful way to bring the needs of others before God.

In addition to these practical tools, you can also pray for others in their daily lives, and offer those acts of kindness or even your daily tasks for their intentions. This can be done through simple acts of kindness, such as offering a kind word or a listening ear, or through more formal acts of intercession, such as writing letters or making phone calls to those in need. To pray more for others, it is essential to have a heart that is open and attentive to the needs of those around us. This requires us to be mindful of the struggles and challenges that others face and to be willing to offer our support and comfort through our prayers.

By using tools such as the Rosary, novenas, and intercession in Mass, we can offer prayers for the needs of others and become more selfless, as what we gain out of it is to grow in virtue and love of others while assisting them. It really is a two-edged sword!

Chapter 10

Professional prestige – why we work

OPUS Dei's founder, St Josemaría Escrivá, emphasised the value of holiness in one's professional life. He professed that one may advance professionally while upholding a fervent Catholic faith and that our secular work and personal sanctity are not incompatible.

> *"Your ordinary contact with God takes place where your fellow men, your yearnings, your work and your affections are. There you have your daily encounter with Christ. It is in the midst of the most material things of the earth that we must sanctify ourselves, serving God and all mankind," (Conversations, 113).*

Here are three useful resources that can aid in your career advancement and growth in professional prestige to grow in holiness and glorify God:

1. Make an effort to do your best work and to be the best at what you do. One of the basic tenets of St

Josemaría's teachings is the pursuit of perfection in one's job. You may show your dedication to your career and elevate your status by always attempting to become the best at your profession, by doing your finest work.

2. Build a strong work ethic. Another strategy to improve your professional standing is to cultivate a strong working attitude. This entails being punctual, trustworthy, and willing to go beyond what is required to attain the outcome that is desired.

3. Network and establish connections. Developing connections with colleagues and business leaders can help you advance your career. You may learn important lessons, discover new chances, and enhance your professional reputation through networking and forming partnerships. Remember that we are also working to serve our fellow brothers and sisters around us in our professional work, as well as our families for whom we work for in many cases.

Chapter II

Sanctifying your work

FINDING holiness in one's everyday job can be a challenge, but as Catholics, we are called to bring God into all aspects of our lives, including our work. A job, no matter how small or seemingly insignificant, can be a source of sanctification if we approach it with the right attitude.

Pope Benedict XVI reminded us of this importance in his apostolic exhortation, *Verbum Domini*:

> *"The Christian life is essentially marked by an encounter with Jesus Christ, who calls us to follow him," (Verbum Domini, 72).*

Because Christ is the master of all and gives nothing away, we must therefore encourage others to follow Him.

Here are a few ways a Catholic might make their work holy and discover holiness in their routine tasks:

1. Offer your work to God. This straightforward but effective gesture can give your work a tremendous deal of meaning. Every day, give your labour to God, asking that He will bless it and utilise it for His glory. This act of dedication can calm you down on a difficult day and help you see your work as a form of prayer.

2. Keep in mind the blessings God has given you. We should be thankful for the abilities, talents and skills that God has given us. You can discover meaning and fulfilment in your career by thinking about these talents and how you can apply them.

3. Seek opportunities to serve others. Seeking out opportunities to serve others is one of the most crucial methods to achieve holiness in your work. Serving others can be very fulfilling and joyful at work, whether it's assisting a teammate with a task or going above and beyond for a customer.

4. Do your work well for the sake of Christ. Serve others all for the sake of Our Lord as if you are doing him a personal favour in the literal sense.

5. Talk of Christ in your work. That is to simply do an effective apostolate, by finding opportunities in a natural way to speak about Christ through a conversation in a professional atmosphere.

The greatest tragedy for members of the laity is to compartmentalise their faith until Sunday Mass or times at church. We must be living our faith always and in every ordinary circumstance. The pursuit of holiness in one's work is not only attainable but also essential to the Catholic faith. We may bring God into every area of our lives and find joy and peace in our work if we approach it with the correct mindset, give it up to God, serve others, be mindful and cultivate a positive outlook.

Chapter 12

Fighting racism today

"RESPECT for the human person entails respect for the rights that flow from his dignity as a creature. These rights are prior to society and must be recognised by it," (Catechism of the Catholic Church, Paragraph 1930).

It is therefore clear that our faith compels us to love all people, because we are all created in His image and likeness, with no exceptions! Racism is a destructive force that distracts us from God's creative work. It creates division, promotes hate and dehumanises those targeted by it. To put an end to racism, it is crucial that we take proactive steps in our everyday lives to promote authentic unity and equality. The Catholic faith is the ultimate antidote to racism, because we are a 'Catholic' or 'universal' Church for all peoples of the earth.

Learning more about racism's effects on our society and raising our awareness are the first steps in combating racism. Read books, watch documentaries, go to workshops and seminars and have deep conversations with individuals from other backgrounds to address any biases we may personally have against a group.

The ability to speak out against racism whenever and wherever we see it is a crucial component of the battle against racism. This may entail rejecting racist comments or jokes and defending those who are the target of discrimination in our workplaces. Fostering relationships with individuals from all backgrounds is a potent weapon against bigotry. Reaching out to those who are different from us and consciously attempting to understand their viewpoints and experiences can help with this.

Here are three practical tools to take action against racism:

1. Raise people's awareness through friendship that God created all of us equal and that racism is really a waste of time and a serious distraction from loving everyone and advancing humanity and the Gospel.

2. Support diversity in organisations. Encourage all people to apply for positions in organisations, to better increase the chances of diversity. Remember, individuals should never be hired or placed in positions of power to fill a diversity quota. Rather, we should promote a healthy opportunity for everyone to have a chance of entering an organisation or a leadership position, where there will be a diverse range of people, and where we focus on their skill set and character.

3. Friendship with others from different cultures can help us better appreciate and understand them. Also, having our friends connected with different people and being a bridge-builder ourselves can help to unite all people of different backgrounds.

Although combating racism is a difficult and constant effort, motivated Christians have a special chance to have a constructive influence. We may encourage understanding and fairness and work to develop a more just and equitable society by educating ourselves, standing up for what we believe in and forming partnerships.

Chapter 13

Faith and food

For physical and mental wellbeing, it is crucial to establish a positive connection with food as a source of nourishing the human body. Therefore, we must treat the body like a temple and learn to eat proportionately and avoid gluttony.

Gluttony as the excessive indulgence in food or drink could have negative consequences on one's spiritual life.

The body is the temple of the Holy Spirit, and as such, deserves to be treated with respect and care. According to what the Church teaches, we have a responsibility to take good care of our bodies and foster our physical, mental and spiritual wellbeing. Healthy routines include conducting regular exercise, having adequate amounts of sleep and eating a balanced diet.

Here are three practical tools to take action towards a healthy relationship with food and a balanced lifestyle which you can begin doing today or help others with:

1. Eating with awareness. Eating with awareness can support a healthy relationship with food. This entails focusing on the meal, enjoying every mouthful and observing physical signs of hunger and fullness. By being in the present, we may tune out distractions and unfavourable food thoughts and concentrate on the nutritious qualities of the meal we are eating.

2. Meal preparation. Preparing your meals can help you develop a structured eating strategy and lower your risk of binge eating or undereating. This entails organising meals and snacks ahead of time, making sure they are balanced and contain a range of nutrients. Meal planning also gives you the chance to include nutritious meals and avoid processed and junk food.

3. Mortification or self-denial in the area of eating food is absolutely essential for you to regulate other carnal pleasures such as chastity. If one cannot deny themselves food, how can one then proceed to reject other sins of the flesh and other subsequent sins?

Chapter 14

Bringing someone back to church

As a Catholic, it is a noble and important goal to help a friend who has strayed from the faith to come back to the Church and grow in a deeper relationship with God.

> *"From this loving knowledge of Christ springs the desire to proclaim Him, to 'evangelise', and to lead others to the 'yes' of faith in Jesus Christ,"* (Catechism of the Catholic Church, Paragraph 429).

In summary, our love of God and relationship with Him should be so vibrant that our love overflows like a fountain beyond just ourselves and towards others. It is towards others that we must look to proclaim the Gospel, but only after we have experienced it ourselves, we would therefore naturally be compelled to do so. For we cannot give to others what we do not have ourselves!

Below are some practical tools which will aid you in taking action in the area of bringing someone back to the faith, which in this day and age seems to be the most common form of evangelisation:

1. Listen to their experience of faith. Always ensure you listen to the reason as to why they do not practise the Catholic faith any longer. Be there as a friend for them and build trust and respect between each other.

2. Discuss your personal faith journey. This may be a very effective way to persuade someone to give God a second chance. Describe how your faith has helped you overcome obstacles and given your life a feeling of calm and purpose. As described in 1 Peter 3:15, you must always be ready to give an explanation, so know your theology and apologetics before venturing on your apostolic endeavour.

3. Friendship. Build a constant and fruitful friendship built upon good human virtue and other activities which are not faith-based. Build friendship in its simplicity!

It's also crucial to keep in mind that restoring someone's faith is a lengthy process that might take some time. Be patient and keep encouraging and supporting them. By listening and empathising, sharing your own religious experience, encouraging them to give God a second chance and come back to Church, you may not see results immediately, but you are surely planting a seed, and it may have even started to grow under the soil!

Chapter 15

The art of humility

LIVING humility is a crucial aspect of personal growth and relationships with others, and more importantly imitating Christ, and essentially becoming more human! It involves recognising one's limitations, embracing one's flaws and being open to learning and growth. One can also fall into a false humility from the other end of the spectrum, which doubts or degrades oneself constantly, in order to humble oneself, as opposed to thanking God for his blessings in one's life while not becoming prideful at the same time. Humility is a nice balance.

St Thomas Aquinas teaches:

> *"Though the virtue of humility cannot attach to Christ in His divine nature; it may attach to Him in His human nature and His divinity renders His humility all the more praiseworthy, for the dignity of the person adds to the merit of humility; and there can be no greater dignity to a man than his being God. Hence the highest*

> *praise attaches to the humility of the Man God, who to wean men's hearts from worldly glory to the love of divine glory, chose to embrace a death of no ordinary sort, but a death of the deepest ignominy," (Summa Contra Gent., tr. Rickaby, bk. IV. ch. lv).*

Here are three practical tools to help cultivate humility in your daily life:

1. Cultivate thankfulness. By turning one's attention away from oneself and towards others, gratitude is a potent strategy that may help promote humility. Set aside some time each day to think about the things for which you are thankful.

2. Setting aside our own ideas and opinions at times and focusing on others and the value that they bring. Therefore, we must die constantly to ourselves for the sake of others.

3. Accept your flaws and your failures. Grow comfortable through spiritual direction. Understand that you are not the best at everything at all times. Be comfortable that you are not the greatest and acknowledge that God is the one who strengthens you.

In conclusion, we must abandon ourselves into Christ, as He demonstrates in His very incarnation and on the cross true humility. We must take action every day, as the root of all evil is pride, we must always be conscious of this to mould ourselves throughout our lives.

Chapter 16

Don't become complacent

CHRISTIAN complacency is detrimental to the growth of your relationship with God. It is easy to fall into the trap of taking our prayer routine and the living out of our faith for granted. However, it is crucial to remain vigilant and avoid complacency in order to deepen our relationship with God and better serve those around us, especially in a world today where we are bored and want to persist with the things which provide us constant pleasure and entertainment.

Here are three practical ways to combat complacency and move forward in our spiritual lives:

1. Regular attendance at Mass and participation in the sacraments are integral to our spiritual lives. We need to understand that we will not 'feel' like doing this every day or week. Also, we will not 'feel' God's consolation or that we are making progress. However, we just need to be consistent and do our best every day to grow more and more, and then over the long

run we will see gradual growth in our spiritual life. So do not expect quick results!

2. Have a personal and human conversation with Jesus Christ every single day. It could mean greeting Our Lord in a meeting, and being conscious that He is with you at all times. This will personalise your spiritual life – after all, the Word did become flesh.

3. Find a group of people who pray together and meet to discuss faith and grow in fraternity. You may carry out acts of charity, which help you to see Christ in your personal relationship with others. After all, we are in communion with one another for a reason.

These tools support us in maintaining vigilance and intentionality in our spiritual lives so we can deepen our faith and serve people in our community more effectively.

Chapter 17

Don't become overzealous

In our eagerness to deepen our spiritual lives, it can be easy to become overly zealous and burn out spiritually and personally. In order to maintain a healthy spiritual life, it's important to find a balance between challenging oneself and sustainability over the long-term.

Here are three practical tools to help you to take action in this crucial area which many people attest to struggle with in our day and age:

1. Practice self-care. It's essential to look after your physical and emotional wellbeing if you want to have a healthy and consistent spiritual life. This includes getting adequate sleep, a nutritious diet, exercise, and taking part in relaxing activities. To avoid burnout, it's also critical to set time aside every week to reflect and take some time to yourself.

2. Establish realistic goals. While it's wonderful to have objectives and plans for your spiritual life, it's crucial to do so, especially during seasons like Lent or Advent. Start out slowly and progressively and challenge yourself gradually. Making steady progress is preferable, rather than giving up on a consistent prayer life after several months because you pushed yourself too far and decided to give up.

3. Seek support. Building and maintaining a healthy spiritual life can be challenging. Try to keep all your activities discreet and don't flaunt your spiritual activities or progress. It is important also to sense when you are becoming overzealous and cut back on steps you otherwise might take. This can be discerned with a spiritual director.

Remember always to set realistic goals and seek support guided by a spiritual director so that the fuel of love may propel you forward, and the practical steps you take should always be proportionate. So, allow love to be your fuel which propels you forward, and the prayers and spiritual steps you take are the gears which you shift into.

Chapter 18

Preparing for Lent

LENT is a time of spiritual reflection, sacrifice, and growth for the faithful. This is an annual opportunity to enter into the desert with Jesus and to emulate His life during this time. This is a time which should not be taken lightly and should be used to grow. Here are some tips to help you prepare for Lent and make the most of this season of repentance:

1. Establish precise objectives. Have a detailed strategy for how you will carry out your objectives, whether you wish to increase your charity giving, enhance your prayer life, or give up a particular sin.

2. Become more prayerful. Lent is the perfect time to concentrate on your prayer habit. Try scheduling a definite prayer time each day, such as before or after meals or before going to bed. You may also give another type of prayer a try, such as *Lectio Divina*, the Rosary, or contemplative prayer.

3. Almsgiving is a significant component of Lent. Think about donating money to a good cause, offering your time to assist others, or just being more aware of the needs of people close to you.

4. Regularly attending Mass throughout Lent will help you enhance your spiritual life and deepen your connection with God. Make it a point to go to Mass every Sunday and, if you can, during the week as well.

5. Read the Bible and consider it. Lent is a wonderful time to read the Bible and consider it, particularly the Gospels. To better understand the Gospel's message and how it relates to your life, try reading one chapter a day, starting with the Gospels.

6. Confess all of your sins: Making a good confession is a crucial part of Lent because it gives you the chance to own up to your mistakes, beg for pardon, and accept the priest's absolution. Start Lent on Ash Wednesday with confession, and plan to go to confession frequently throughout Lent.

7. Ask a spiritual mentor for advice. If you have a spiritual mentor or spiritual director, think about asking them for advice during Lent. They may be a great source of encouragement and keep you focused on your spiritual objectives.

8. Exercise self-control. When we make sacrifices and work to advance our spiritual selves, Lent is a time of self-control. Even when things get difficult, keep your attention on your goals and try to avoid distractions.

In conclusion, Lent is a time to focus on spiritual development by entering into the desert with Our Lord and allowing Him to shape you in these 40 days. This is a time which should have some permanent effect on you after it has ended. If you have chosen to attend daily Mass during Lent, for example, then you should perhaps continue this every other day for the rest of the year to come. There should be some growth out of each Lenten season.

Chapter 19

Setting and keeping your New Year's goals

A FANTASTIC approach to begin the new year with a good perspective and a strategy for development and progress is to set New Year's goals. To improve the likelihood of success beyond the month of January, your goals should be concise and very realistic.

Break up your goals into four categories:

1. Spiritual: All things relating to your faith and spiritual life.

2. Physical: All things relating to your bodily health and presentation.

3. Work: All this relates to your career, investments or any other side hustles to do with providing for yourself or professional development.

4. Social: All things relating to your relationships with your spouse, family, friends and networks.

Ensure that your goals for each are few and are attainable. What is often helpful is to assign a review date for each of your goals after every quarter. During this time, you may want to work on several goals at the same time. Or you may wish to work on each aspect of life and its respective goal for that particular quarter of the year.

Chapter 20

Preparing for the month of All Souls

Praying for the dead during the month of All Souls, which falls in November, is a great deed towards those who have departed. One should petition for the intercession of their deceased loved ones in heaven during this month and be on the lookout for their spiritual wellbeing. We can still pray for the dead and receive their prayers in return, because death is not the end, but rather a passage to eternal life.

As the expression *'memento mori'* implies, thinking about our own mortality is a crucial aspect of getting ready for the month of All Souls and allowing this to shape the way we wake up on every other day of the year. It serves as a reminder that we should spend our lives in a way that pleases God, since one day we shall all pass away, and in many cases, we may not know when this may happen. This reflection can assist us in setting priorities for what is most crucial in life and in leading meaningful lives.

Here are three practical tools that can help you to prepare for the month of All Souls and the rest of the year, and to facilitate the contemplation of our own mortality:

1. Reciting the Rosary is one of the most meritorious and effective methods to pray for the deceased. You can do this devotion alone or with a group, reciting prayers and reflecting on the mysteries of Jesus' and Mary's lives, while paying attention to the words: "and at the hour of our death".

2. A cemetery visit may be a moving opportunity to remember and pray for the deceased during the month of All Souls. It will help to ingrain the reality of our own mortality in our mind, because we are present where many are buried. It can help to kick us back into the reality that we need to pray for the departed.

3. Making an offering. Another practical way to prepare for the month of All Souls is to offer up a Mass for the faithful departed and to be specific with the names of those who have left us. We should also offer other penances during the month of All Souls and during every other month, to stay united to the faithful departed and to never allow us to forget our eventual mortality.

Finally, praying for the dead achieves two things. It benefits those souls who are in purgatory and require our prayers, but it also helps us at the same time to keep focused on our mortality, thereby allowing us to remain vigilant against sin and to desire to grow closer to God, who we shall return to at the end of our lives.

Chapter 21

Preparing for Advent

ADVENT is a time of penance and preparation for the birth of Our Lord, and this should not be distracted by the hype and consumerism of our time. It is a period for similar penance to Lent, and spiritual development in preparation for Christ to take flesh in the world and most importantly, our own lives.

Advent preparations according to tradition:

1. Fasting and abstinence. Fast during the time leading up to Christmas as you would for Lent. Make a similar plan to Lent.

2. Use of the Advent wreath. The Advent wreath is a classic seasonal sign composed of evergreens and lit by four candles to commemorate each of the four weeks of Advent. Each week, a single candle is lit to represent the advent of Christ and the light shining

in the darkness. Keep one in a visible location in your house throughout this time of year.

3. Advent prayers and devotions. Catholics can also prepare for Advent through special prayers and devotions, such as the Angelus, the Rosary, or the St Andrew novena. Additionally, many parishes offer special Advent prayers and devotions, such as an Advent penance service or an Advent mission, which can help Catholics to deepen their spiritual lives during this special season.

Here are some practical tools to take you through Advent:

1. Anticipate the coming of Christ every morning during this time.

2. Giving back. As Advent draws to a close, Catholics should continue to give back, whether it is through volunteering, making a donation, or simply being kind to those who are in need.

3. Lastly, as Advent draws to a close, Catholics should take some time to consider their spiritual journey and develop a strategy for ongoing spiritual growth and renewal. This might entail adopting new spiritual resolutions, going on a retreat, or just resolving to engage in daily prayer and devotion.

Let us prepare for this special season in meaningful and significant ways, through traditional practices like fasting and abstinence, the use of the Advent wreath, and special prayers and devotions. We must welcome Christ to become flesh in our lives so that we may become another Christ to the world and draw men to Him.

Chapter 22

Embracing liturgical feasts

LET'S discuss how we might more intentionally observe the specific saints' feast days in our daily lives. We frequently pass by feast days in our missals and we can often be tempted not to discover the saint who is behind that particular day. We may strengthen our devotion, become closer to God, and preach the Gospel by paying tribute to the saints. The saints, martyrs and other holy men and women who are included in the memorials, feasts and solemnities are effective intercessors who we can often relate to in their life story.

1. Go to Mass. Attend Mass on the day of the saint you are honouring, if you can. This is a wonderful method to strengthen your bond with the saints and express gratitude for their intercession.

2. Read the saint's life. Study the saint you are honouring by reading about their life and their writings. This will help you comprehend their lives and the lessons they have for us better.

3. Become grateful. Ask the saint you are honouring for their intercession in a particular area of help they are known for. Remember, there are many patrons for different areas of life.

4. Make a shrine. Construct a modest shrine to the saint you are commemorating, filling it with a picture, candles, and other mementoes of the saint's legacy. This may be a wonderful approach to strengthen your love for them and invite them into your house.

5. Tell the story. Tell people, especially if you have children, about the saint you are commemorating. This is a fantastic approach to advance the Gospel and preserve the heritage of the saints.

6. Fast. In order to be closer to God, several saints observed fasts. As a way to emulate the saint you are celebrating, think about fasting on their feast day.

7. Family celebration. Invite your family to join you in celebrating the saint's feast day. Cook a particular meal to bring attention to that particular saint. These small efforts can often go a long way in your devotional life.

Chapter 23

Overcoming habitual sin

We all understand how difficult it may be to break bad habits of sin. It is crucial to first comprehend what habitual sin is. Sinful behaviour that repeats itself and gets ingrained in our everyday life is referred to as habitual sin. This might range from deception and fraud to drug misuse and addiction. Because it is simpler to succumb to temptation each time we participate in the behaviour, habitual sin is a slippery slope. It is crucial to strive towards conquering the sin because of this.

Recognising your chronic sin is the first step in overcoming it. We must accept responsibility for our actions and see the behaviour for what it is. This necessitates humility and an openness to being truthful with God and ourselves. Our first step towards improvement might be to recognise the issue and confess our faults to a priest or a reliable friend.

Accountability is a crucial component in overcoming a bad habit. This entails establishing a network of encouraging friends and family members who will uplift us and keep us responsible for our behaviour. We might also want to think about engaging with a therapist or spiritual director who can assist us in figuring out the origins of our behaviour and creating a strategy for change.

Thirdly, it's critical to persist in our efforts to break free from recurring sin. It will take a lot of perseverance and resolve to do this. It's critical to keep in mind that change takes time and that roadblocks are commonplace in the course of development. Even when we feel dejected or disheartened, we must be kind to ourselves and keep looking to God for help.

Here are three overarching practical strategies which can help you phase out any habitual sin within your life:

1. Establishing a daily pattern of prayer and contemplation might include morning and evening prayers. It is vital to have a plan for our life that we intend to live by, so that we do not leave our prayer life to the chance of the changing environment of our day. It must be solidified in an itinerary-like schedule so that we make less room for temptation.

2. Find a supportive network. Join a small group or find a spiritual director to help you with the spiritual aspects of your problem.

3. Create a change plan. Establish a strategy for change by discussing your sin's underlying causes with a professional therapist in addition to your spiritual director. Setting clear objectives, replacing immoral behaviours with new interests or pursuits, and asking dependable friends or family members for accountability are a few examples of how to do this.

Nothing is impossible by the grace of God in overcoming habitual sin. It requires acceptance of the issue, a strengthening of one's connection with God through prayer, accountability and proactivity. Keep in mind that transformation takes time and that there will be obstacles on the road, which will form part of your progress, only if you use them as a stepping stone to grow your conviction and resolve. Keep your faith and keep looking to Our Lord for help and encouragement.

Chapter 24

The art of mortification

"A SPIRIT *of mortification, rather than being just an outward show of Love, arises as one of its consequences. If you fail in one of these little proofs, acknowledge that your love for the Love is wavering,'* (St Josemaría Escrivá, Furrow, 981).

Mortification is the act of willingly enduring discomfort for the purpose of spiritual development, inspired by the love of God, and undertaken as a form of self-discipline. It is a method of letting go of one's ego and selfish desires in order to grow closer to Christ and receive more of His grace.

Mortification entails giving up our own will and wants as well as depriving ourselves of bodily pleasure. In order to be more focused on serving God and others, it is a method of saying "no" to our ego and our own desires, with the underlying fuel of the love of God. Similar to the scenario of wanting to go to the gym every day in order to build a strong physique, motivated by the underlying goal, someone may strive to push their endurance and endure much pain and torn muscles, but for the ultimate goal of achieving the reward of a great physique. Likewise, we need to push our spiritual endurance in a similar manner by disciplining our bodies to achieve a great spiritual physique.

Here are some practical tools to take action in this crucial area:

1. Fasting is the first strategy. Fasting is a sort of self-denial that lessens reliance on material possessions and promotes spiritual growth. Through fasting, you may develop self-control over your body and cravings while sharpening your attention on God and His plan.

2. Self-control is another useful skill. This entails exercising control over my thoughts and deeds in order to develop more virtue and become nearer to God. Instead of engaging in immoral behaviour, try to make an effort to focus on doing good deeds and cultivating virtues like patience, humility and compassion. Spend time with people who uplift you and help you to build good human virtue.

3. Mortify your will. It can be often effortless for many Catholics to fast from food, water and television. However, take up the challenge of mortifying your everyday will. For example, if you want to tell a joke with your friends, refrain from it. Furthermore, if you wish to complain about something at work, refrain from it. In conclusion, try to find things you wish to do, which are not necessary, and refrain from doing them.

Chapter 25

How to start a lay apostolate

THE vast majority of the Church is laity! The laity have a unique role to play in the Church, as it is not just the role of the hierarchy to engage in apostolate and to evangelise our culture today, but for all the faithful.

The *Catechism of the Catholic Church* states:

> *"The laity, by their very vocation, seek the kingdom of God by engaging in temporal affairs and by ordering them according to the plan of God," (Paragraph 898).*

You therefore must make a difference in the world and establish God's kingdom by using your skills, interests and passions in your everyday circumstances – at work, in your domestic home and with your friends and other social or political organisations in which you are a part of. One way to achieve this is to launch your own apostolate.

After you have a broad idea of the apostolate you wish to start, you may utilise these three helpful tools to help you move forward:

1. It is essential to pray and discern what God is calling you to do before taking action. Spend some time by yourself and listen to what the Holy Spirit may be telling you over a period of time.

2. Work together. It is difficult to start an apostolate alone, but you don't have to. Locate others who may have the same goal and way of carrying themselves as you, and partner up with them to start an initiative to meet new people who may already be Catholic or not and help them to start discovering Christ in a deeper way. Examples of this can be starting a podcast or a speaking program in a pub or parish to help meet and network with new people, while being centred around an activity like a talk or a reflection.

3. It doesn't have to be a complicated process to begin your apostolate; do it in little steps. Start small and advance gradually. Set realistic goals and engage in actions to realise your vision. Appreciate your minor triumphs along the way to keep your motivation high.

Keep in mind that it is your responsibility as a layperson to spread the Gospel in the temporal sphere. You will be able to attract many souls by carrying out an effective apostolate that is in keeping with your personal style and character. Take the initial step, put your faith in God's direction, and then watch as your apostolate expands and thrives. As Pope Francis says: "Do not be afraid. Take courage. Your work, united with that of all the faithful, will bear much fruit."

Chapter 26

Prepare for the second coming

JESUS will return in the manner foretold in the Gospels and expounded upon in the Book of Revelation. It's crucial to get ready for this second coming in a healthy way, rather than by developing an obsession with doomsday scenarios, as often sells in today's world on social media. Many people often prepare for apocalyptic events by building a bunker in their home, praying for the return of Christ, planning the perfect escape. But the most tragic apocalypse is that they did not prepare for everyday life and God's call in the midst of their daily tasks. It can give you much more of a 'kick' to focus on the apocalypse rather than to look at your prayer life and your relationships in everyday life. That is the biggest devastation of all!

Let us recalibrate our focus and energy for becoming saints in the middle of the world, regardless of when Our Lord returns, so that we will not be moved by fear, but by faith, and that Our Lord can find us doing His will at the moment He returns:

1. Meditate on the second coming of Christ before Mass, and understand that the second coming should not be too different (on a spiritual level) than that of attending Mass. The end time doomsday should not then occupy our minds, if we have already welcomed Our Lord every day, as the second coming is just another day.

2. Minimise all apocalyptic movies, blogs or videos that you would immerse yourself in. If we have a strong prayer life, there is no time to worry about the end times, because we would be preoccupied with growing in holiness, which then overcomes the earthly problems. Think big!

3. Study the Book of Revelation from reputable Catholic sources. My suggestion is to study this in a group, in order to have a concise understanding about the end of time, rather than appeal to the misinterpretations that constantly plague the final book of the New Testament.

Keep in mind that your own spiritual development should take precedence over making predictions about the end of the world or the details of the second coming. You'll be well on your way to being ready for the second coming in a healthy and meaningful way by using these useful tips. You will have spiritually embraced 'Christ's first coming' every day.

Chapter 27

How to become a saint

IT should be everyone's life goal to receive the Nobel Prize of the Catholic faith, which is the salvation of one's soul, ultimately to spend eternity with God. This love overflows in the cases of many saints, who in this life desired heaven for themselves and others. St Therese of Lisieux says:

> *"I want to spend my heaven in doing good on earth,"* (St Therese of Lisieux, The Final Conversations, tr. John Clarke (Washington: ICS, 1977), 102).

We should all aim to be canonised saints. This is the aim of our faith, and there is no other intrinsic purpose. We must not distract ourselves with focuses other than the centre of our life's purpose, which is to love and return to that source of love at the end of our earthly journey.

Here are three practical tools to help you take action now to stay focused on your life's mission of becoming a saint:

1. Prayer routine. The cornerstone of all spiritual development is prayer. It's a means to interact with God, to establish a connection with Him, and to let Him change you on the inside. Set aside regular time each day for personal prayer, try to attend Mass every day, and regularly partake in the sacraments. A daily, weekly or monthly plan should include all of them. It would be dangerous to leave our prayers to chance.

2. Theological study. Studying the principles which guide our daily lives is essential to maintaining the spirit of struggle in our prayer practise and Christian living. Regular reading of Scripture, the Catechism, and other spiritual writings are examples of this. Think about how you can use what you're learning in your life while you study. To keep your knowledge current, think about regularly enrolling in a Bible study group, a formalised course at a respectable and orthodox school, or an unofficial group.

3. Serving others. Growing in holiness is best accomplished through serving others. Service can take many different forms, such as working in your church, volunteering for a charity or paying visits to the sick and elderly. Consider serving others a top priority in your life and look for opportunities to do so.

You will be well on your way to developing holiness and becoming a saint by implementing these tools. Yet, it's crucial to keep in mind that developing holiness is a lifelong process that calls for tenacity, tolerance, and a sincere love for God.

You can take the following extra actions to strengthen your relationship with God and develop your holiness:

1. Develop a strong devotion to Mary, the Virgin Mother of God. She is a strong intercessor and will support your sanctification.

2. Do a daily examination of conscience to consider your deeds and to ask for forgiveness.

3. Choose a spiritual director who can give you advice and direction so you can develop your connection with God.

4. Through fasting, forgoing some comforts, or engaging in additional spiritual activities, exercise self-control and self-denial.

5. Be inspired by particular saints and try to emulate their love for God and their fervent commitment to prayer.

6. Attend retreats, courses, or classes to expand your knowledge of the faith.

7. Feed the hungry, clothe the naked, and visit the ill and incarcerated, among other acts of kindness.

8. Develop the theological virtues of faith, hope and charity, as well as the cardinal virtues of wisdom, justice, fortitude and temperance to live a virtuous life.

9. Getting rid of worldly belongings and focusing only on what is required for your spiritual development can help you live a life of simplicity and detachment.

10. Ultimately, develop a strong love for God and strive to fulfil all of His wishes.

The above are only guidelines for becoming a saint but must ultimately be directed by love. The path to holiness is a lifelong one that requires many sacrifices along the way. With His grace, you may spread the word about His kingdom and influence others to follow Him. Ultimately, the salvation of our souls is not a rule book, but rather our deeper and deeper love of God. However, we as humans always need practical means to conform our wills and hearts so that we can be transformed.

Chapter 28

Staying clear of demonic influence

YOU may sometimes feel that you're under the influence of demonic or occult forces in certain places, with certain music or experiences. This can lead to feelings of fear, anxiety and insecurity. Many people are often fascinated by the work of the demonic, even those with no faith at all. It can be easier to fill a room giving a talk about this topic than that of prayer or any other moral or theological topic. There is something which fascinates people about this area more than others.

Exorcists are often the experts on these matters, particularly Fr Gabriel Amorth, the former exorcist of the Diocese of Rome, who exclaims in his book:

> *"It is necessary to educate them from an early age to cultivate a life of faith through prayer, through the Mass, and through association with the various Catholic youth clubs and other similar organisations. It is absolutely necessary to give them a sense of God and the awareness of the existence of sin and the devil, the tempter who*

wishes to lead us to a separation from God and therefore to death. These young people, then, when they become older, will probably have developed the right attitudes toward these sects and satanic practices. I am aware that it involves a difficult form of education, but let us always remember that, because of the total absence of beautiful and good ideals, young people today are more exposed to these dangers. When faith disappears, one abandons himself to superstition and occultism," (An Exorcist Explains the Demonic: The Antics of Satan and His Army of Fallen Angels).

Apart from the usual spiritual plan that has been discussed in previous chapters, additional things to distance oneself from the demonic influence below can be employed:

1. Use sacramentals weekly, such as the St Benedict medal (blessed only with the prescribed prayer by a priest), wearing the scapular (installed only with the correct prayer by a priest) and exorcised holy water and salt.

2. Enshrine your prayer routine, as per Chapter 27.

3. Bless all items in your house. Rid all decorations or items which are intrinsically evil, or false idols and statues or images associated with other deities. These could be items which may have been bought from places which have been associated with the occult, especially antique stores which were owned by other people before. This can even extend to types of music which you have purchased and the lyrics they contain.

4. Get advice from your local diocesan exorcist for any concerns that may be troubling you. It may be a good idea for you to meet your local exorcist for spiritual direction, because they may have a unique perspective to guide you in your spiritual life, as they have experienced the demonic first-hand.

By following these steps and using these practical tools, you can overcome demonic or occult influences in your life and reclaim your spiritual power as a Catholic. Remember, demonic influence is not the greatest tragedy, it is ultimately losing your soul. Our goal is never to be scared or intimidated by any demonic influence, we are focused on the salvation of our soul, and winning other souls to Christ.

Chapter 29

Explore the Eastern Churches

You have a special chance to broaden your spiritual horizons by attending Eastern Catholic rites as a member of the Catholic Church. The Catholic Church, which is the universal Church, is made up of several distinct self-governing churches which celebrate their own liturgical rites, each of which has a rich historical, cultural and spiritual background.

According to the Second Vatican Council's decree on the Eastern Churches, *Orientalium Ecclesiarum*, Eastern Catholic Churches have the right to preserve their liturgical and spiritual traditions and members of the Western Catholic Church are encouraged to experience these traditions.

Here are three practical tools, which are very easy, for you to immerse yourself in Eastern Catholic life, and experience the "second lung" which the Church breathes from, according to St Pope John Paul II:

1. Research. Start by researching the various Eastern Catholic rites and their locations within your city, and also other cities which you may be visiting.

2. Plan. Once you have a list of rites which you want to experience, do your research on each of these rites and their history. I recommend watching a video and reading the ritual book of the liturgy itself, which would prepare you to easily attend that particular Eastern Church.

3. Connect. Book an appointment if possible with the local priest or community of that rite for a tour of the church and the community some time before the liturgy or after. This would help to strengthen the morale of those communities, to show support to the Eastern Churches in being proud and sharing their tradition, as exhorted by the Second Vatican Council.

4. To better understand the diversity present in the liturgical rites of the Eastern Church, one must refer back to the Latin rite itself, and seek to experience the other rites within the Latin Church. For example, the Traditional Latin Mass (1962), Ordinariate Use of the Roman Rite, the Dominican Rite, the Ambrosian Rite, the Mozarabic Rite and many other rites just within the framework of the Latin Church. This would better help many in the West to understand how we are able to be one Church and yet have many liturgical ways to celebrate the same Eucharist.

You can start a journey to learn more about the Catholic Church's rich spiritual legacy and to strengthen your faith by following these steps. Whether you decide to attend one rite or several, you will undoubtedly be moved by the Eastern Catholic rites' lovely traditions and the variety of the universal Church. Most importantly, you will experience how a diversity of liturgical rites are all the same Eucharistic Sacrifice.

Chapter 30

Catholic political influence

It is the laity's duty to introduce the ideals and tenets of their religion into the political sphere. In addition to protecting everyone's dignity and providing for the most vulnerable members of society, we must advance the common good. The policies and choices made by our elected leaders ought to be based on these principles, and it is our responsibility as laypeople to see to it that they are.

We may advocate for the social doctrine of the Church and expand its civil freedoms in a number of ways. Running for office, backing a political party or just exercising one's right to vote are many ways to get active in politics.

Here are practical tips to help you take action in this area:

1. Learn about political candidates and problems. This is the most crucial and initial step in entering politics. Knowing the problems that concern your neighbourhood and the stances of the candidates for

office are crucial. You may accomplish this by phoning the candidate's office directly and, if possible, setting up a meeting to evaluate them in person.

2. Join forces with groups and individuals that share your interests. A wonderful method to connect with others who share your ideas is by joining a political party and lobby group that you support. For anyone interested in running for office or working on political campaigns, these organisations frequently offer training and support.

3. Think about vying for office or backing a political candidate. It's a terrific approach to improve your community and advance your Catholic principles in public policy to run for office. Even if you decide not to run for office yourself, it is nonetheless crucial to support political candidates whose views are similar to your own. This may be accomplished by working in campaigns, offering financial support or educating friends and family members about the value of voting.

4. Voting is a right that you should use, and you should also urge others to vote. One of the most effective methods to influence the political process is by voting. Make sure you are registered to vote, be knowledgeable about the topics and encourage others in your community to use their right to vote.

5. Pray for direction and discernment in your political choices. Ultimately, it's critical to keep in mind that your faith should inform your political decisions. Pray for direction and discernment as you navigate the political environment and look for chances to share the compassion and love of Christ there.

Chapter 31

Pick up your Bible

SCRIPTURE is the written word of God under the inspiration of the Holy Spirit. The *Catechism of the Catholic Church* states:

> "Sacred Scripture is the speech of God as it is put down in writing under the breath of the Holy Spirit," (Paragraph 81).

It is therefore imperative that we be immersed in it and know it better than any other book. We also thank God for the Tradition and most especially the Magisterium of the Church.

Here are some practical ways to take action in this area:

1. Establish a timetable. It's crucial to establish a regular plan for reading the Bible. A routine can help you keep to your objective, whether it's every morning, every evening or at a set time during the day. Make it a top priority and include it in your list of daily tasks.

You'll be less likely to forget or become distracted by other activities and more likely to finish your reading.

2. Employ a Bible reading plan. You may find Bible reading programs online or in actual Bibles. They provide you with a methodical technique to study the Bible and monitor your progress. Choose a strategy that works for you and follow it. Having a plan can help you remain on track and ensure that you read the entire Bible, whether you want to read a little bit every day or more on the weekends.

3. Find a study partner or group. Reading the Bible with a friend or in a Bible study group may make the experience more pleasant and less daunting. Locate a friend who wants to read the Bible, then plan to meet together and talk about what you've read. This could take place in-person, on the phone, or even via video chat. You'll stay motivated and on track if you have someone to talk to and hold you accountable.

You'll be well on your way to reading the entire Bible easily and conveniently if you use these three resources. Keep in mind that reading the Bible is a lifetime endeavour, so don't be disheartened if you get behind. Simply go on from where you left off.

Chapter 32

What is manhood?

You have a duty to live a life of faith, honesty, and service to others as a Catholic man, most especially in this period of time. Being a Catholic man means making a commitment to your spiritual and personal development, as well as your readiness to live out your faith in the real world. A career that requires you to finally die to yourself.

Start by developing a close relationship with God through prayer and devotion. This can be accomplished through engaging in sacramental practices, frequent attendance at Mass and daily prayer and meditation. Moreover, you might want to think about enrolling in a men's group or attending a retreat to foster a sense of community and support among Catholic men.

Serving others as a way to live out your religion is another facet of being a Catholic man. This can take many different forms, such as working at a neighbourhood food bank, mentoring young people or going on a humanitarian mission trip. You not only assist others by acting on your faith, but you also strengthen your personal connection with God.

The development of values like humility, empathy, and respect for others is also crucial. This entails treating everyone you come into contact with respect and compassion, even when it's challenging. It also entails appreciating sacrifice and prioritising the needs of others over your own.

Consider adopting the following resources into your life to take action in this area:

1. Daily prayer and meditation. Set aside some time each day to think about your religion and get closer to God. This can be accomplished by prayer, reading from the Bible or other peaceful spiritual exercises.

2. Search for chances to help others, whether it is by volunteering in your town, contributing to regional causes, or going on mission trips. You will further your own spiritual development and spread the love of Christ to others by putting your faith into practice.

3. Developing virtues. Focus on acquiring traits like respect for others, humility and empathy. This may be accomplished through regularly engaging in self-reflection and self-improvement, as well as by looking to spiritual mentors and role models for assistance.

You may truly and significantly live out your Catholic masculinity by adopting these skills into your life. You may strengthen your relationship with God and spread love and hope to people around you by praying, serving others and developing your virtues.

Chapter 33

A Rite of Passage to Manhood

A RITE of passage is a significant event or series of events that mark a transition from one stage of life to another. For Christian men, the rite of passage to manhood is a transformative experience that helps them to grow in their faith and become the men God has called them to be. In this chapter, we will explore the concept of a rite of passage to manhood in the Christian context and provide five practical ways that a young boy, teenager or man can create a rite of passage for himself.

The Importance of a Rite of Passage to Manhood

A rite of passage to manhood is important for Christian men because it helps them understand their role and responsibilities as men of God. It also helps them develop a stronger sense of identity and purpose, and provides them with a sense of belonging to a community of men who share their beliefs and values. Furthermore, a rite of passage to manhood can help Christian men develop spiritual maturity, emotional intelligence, and a strong sense of self-worth.

The Christian View of Manhood

According to the Bible, manhood is defined by the characteristics of courage, strength, wisdom and humility. A man is called to be a leader, a protector and a provider for his family and community. He is also called to be a disciple of Jesus Christ and to live a life of holiness, obedience and service to others. In order to become the man God has called him to be, a Christian man must undergo a process of growth and transformation that is rooted in his faith in Jesus Christ.

Five practical ways to create a rite of passage to manhood

1. Spend time in prayer and Bible study. One of the most important aspects of a rite of passage to manhood is a deep and personal relationship with God. This can be cultivated through regular prayer and Bible study. By setting aside time each day to pray and read the Bible, a young boy, teenager or man can develop a closer relationship with God and gain the wisdom and strength he needs to live a life of courage and service to others.

2. Engage in physical activities. Physical activities such as sports, exercise and outdoor adventures can help to develop strength, courage and perseverance. By challenging himself physically, a young boy, teenager or man can also develop a sense of self-worth and gain a deeper appreciation for the power and potential of his body.

3. Serve others. Another important aspect of a rite of passage to manhood is a commitment to serve others. By volunteering for local charities, helping out in the community or simply being there for a friend in need,

one can learn the value of putting others first and develop a sense of empathy and compassion.

4. Spend time with older and wiser men. Spending time with older men who have already gone through a rite of passage to manhood can provide valuable guidance and support. By listening to their stories, asking questions and learning from their experiences, a young boy or teenager can gain a deeper understanding of what it means to be a man of God and the challenges and triumphs that come with that journey.

5. Participate in a mentorship program. Finally, participating in a mentorship program can provide a structured and supportive environment to grow and develop as a man of God. By working with a mentor who is further along in his journey, one can gain valuable insights, guidance and support as he embarks on his own rite of passage to manhood.

Chapter 34

Rites and rituals to grow your faith

THERE is a Latin phrase relating to prayer, belief and living the faith which is often heard by many. In this context of discussing the importance and relevance of Church rituals, it can provide us with much clarity and understanding to better make sense of them and grow in our appreciation for them.

The phrase states: '*Lex orandi, lex credendi, lex vivendi*', which translates into English as: 'The law of prayer, is the law of belief, is the law of life'.

Rituals represented through the '*lex orandi*' or 'law of prayer' are representative of what the Church teaches in her doctrine, which is the '*lex credendi*'. Therefore, by living out the dogmatic teachings of the Church through the rituals, we should then be naturally motivated to live our faith in our daily life, '*lex vivendi*'.

To summarise this, we ought to be practising what we are preaching, in both what the rituals represent and by proceeding to living this out in our daily life.

For example, if the priest does not use the prescribed formula for confession, the sacrament does not take effect. It is not sufficient to say that it spiritually happened. We must value and take very seriously the exercise of our rituals, not as a result of mere rigidity and nostalgia, but to ensure the sacraments are made present, and furthermore to ensure they are done with reverence, which then impacts the personal spiritual life of the faithful receiving them.

In summary, the *'lex credendi'*, in addition to the *'lex orandi'*, aids people in exercising their faith in the real world, or *'lex vivendi'*. People are able to internalise the Church's teachings and apply them to their everyday lives by partaking in rituals (*lex vivendi*).

There are various useful instruments that people might utilise in order to carry out the *'lex vivendi'* and behave in accordance with their religion. They consist of:

1. Frequent attendance at Mass is important for maintaining a connection with the Church and receiving the sacraments, both of which are necessary for fostering one's faith and upholding the *'lex vivendi'*.

2. Get a copy of the missal and other liturgical books of the Church to read and study the rites. This is another great way to catechise oneself further.

3. Pray the liturgical and ritual prayers closely. If you are at Mass, pray the prayers of the priest. If you are at a baptism, pray closely with that particular ritual. Give thanks interiorly for the rites of the Church.

Chapter 35

Overcome materialism and consumerism

THE idea that purchasing more things will make us happier is all around us. The truth is that materialism and consumerism only provide fleeting happiness, despite the fact that advertisements, billboards and social media all drive you to spend more. In order to live a meaningful life, it's critical to resist these societal pressures and put your attention on what's important. Here are three useful resources to assist you with acting:

1. Mindfulness and gratitude. Being conscious and grateful is the first step towards eliminating consumerism. This entails being mindful of the current moment and appreciative of your possessions. Consider making time each day to think about your blessings, such as your health, your relationships or your possibilities. You'll notice that you feel more pleased and satisfied with your life when you concentrate on the things you have, rather than the things you lack.

2. Re-evaluate your priorities. Take a step back after that and reassess your priorities. What do you appreciate most in life and what is actually essential to you? This might be anything that is important to you, such as your relationships, health, personal development or anything else. Discern for an appropriate amount of time if you wish to purchase something.

3. Make a conscious choice. Last, but not least, decide consciously to end the cycle of consumerism. This entails exercising control over your spending patterns and making decisions that are consistent with your priorities and core beliefs. Begin by making a budget, establishing financial objectives and refraining from impulsive purchases. Choose quality over quantity.

You may transcend materialism and consumerism with the aid of these three strategies and live a more contented life. You may resist the societal pressures that push you to consume more by cultivating mindfulness and thankfulness, reassessing your priorities and making deliberate decisions. You will discover that you have all you need to be content and happy in your life if you keep your attention on what matters most.

Chapter 36

Make sense of Church scandal today

As a Catholic, it can be challenging to balance our belief in Jesus Christ and the Church with the scandals that have broken out inside the Church. It might be easy to get disheartened and lose faith, but it's crucial to keep in mind that even Judas betrayed Jesus and St Peter failed Our Lord, and that the Church is protected by the Holy Spirit.

The following three practical strategies can be beneficial in order to see past the scandals and concentrate on Jesus Christ and His Church:

1. Focus on the positive aspects of the Church. It can be easy to get caught up in the scandals and negative news, but it is important to also focus on the positive aspects of the Church. Your faith should become stronger because we know that it is a divine institution beyond the failings of its leaders. The fact that God can work with fallen humans should actually be seen as great hope.

2. Focus on the sacraments. The sacraments, particularly the Eucharist and Confession, may be a source of support and consolation for us while we are going through a challenging period. They assist in bringing our attention back to Jesus Christ and His Church by serving as a reminder of God's mercy and kindness.

3. Participate in your neighbourhood's and parish's activities to deepen your connection to Jesus Christ and the Church. Become engaged in your local community. Being engaged in your neighbourhood community, whether it be by volunteering, taking part in religious instruction or joining a prayer group, can assist you in concentrating on the good things about the Church and turning away from the scandals.

We may look past the scandals inside the Church and concentrate on Jesus Christ and His Church by focusing on the positive parts of the Church, turning to the sacraments, and being engaged in your local community. Even Judas betrayed Jesus, yet the Holy Spirit protects the Church, so we shouldn't let the scandals demoralise us or lead us to lose faith. Instead, we ought to hold firm to our convictions and keep on following Jesus Christ and His Church.

Chapter 37

Make sense of suffering

Pain and suffering are given ultimate meaning in the death and resurrection of Jesus Christ. Our personal sufferings are given a clear meaning, if God Himself can take on the flesh of humanity and die a very painful and humiliating death. There cannot be more consolation for us as suffering humans as possible, regarding how we can make sense of taking up our personal crosses and follow Christ.

Here are three practical tools about how we can take action with our faith in this very daunting area of embracing and making sense of suffering, to ultimately share in Christ's resurrection:

1. Prayer. Mental or personal prayer is the best way to communicate with God regarding our personal sufferings. Allocating time in the morning and afternoon to speak personally with Christ can propel our embrace of our personal sufferings.

2. Service to others. By becoming selfless, you can learn not to be consumed or absorbed in your own personal problems and look outwards. That is not to say that you do not address your problems at all, but this is a balance that needs to be achieved. So, looking outwards may require you to do charity or seek to help your friends or family with their personal problems and crosses, in a manner that emulates Simon of Cyrene.

3. Gratitude. Giving thanks to God for the blessings of your life by reflecting mentally upon them when you are overcome with sufferings will bring positivity to your personal cross. Looking at your blessings can help sustain you in your resolve to move forward. It is through the cross in the daily lives of many other people that many great achievements are made. These include your personal blessings, which are achieved through carrying your cross. Reflecting on having held your cross before in such circumstances can help you to keep focus on your sanctity, which is coming about as a result of your suffering which God has allowed.

Remember after every crucifixion, there is a resurrection!

Chapter 38

Build authentic friendships

Although it might be difficult to forge genuine friendships in the contemporary world, doing so is essential to our personal development and wellbeing and to support each other in growing in human virtue and faith. Our aspiration of friendship should strive towards a deep friendship to become close companions in life and support one another during good and difficult times.

Constant check-ins with one another are one of the strategies to develop and sustain great friendships. Regular phone conversations, messages or in-person meetings can be used to accomplish this. Setting aside time for more in-depth discussions on life, spirituality and personal development can also help foster this growth in virtue and relationship with one another. A friendship should be more than a casual coffee here and there, it should be a desire to help each other and support each other to grow in human virtue, sanctity and in the temporal achievements. We need a return to greater fraternity among men and women for our age. If one doesn't share the Catholic faith, we are called to love our friends and carry out a personal apostolate with them and meanwhile grow in human virtue.

We may develop a deeper degree of trust and understanding and support one another as we work through any difficulties by often checking in with one another. Here are three useful strategies for creating and sustaining enduring, genuine friendships:

1. Active listening exercises. Active listening is one of the cornerstones to developing healthy relationships. This entails paying close attention to what your friend is saying without interfering or passing judgement. You may convey to your buddy that you appreciate their opinions and feelings by paying close attention to them and engaging them in conversation.

2. Participate in one another's interests. Participating in activities together, whether they include a shared pastime, a sports team or volunteer work, may boost your friendship. Togetherness offers opportunity for enjoyment and relaxation as well as new and distinct perspectives on each other.

3. Be honest and vulnerable. Honesty and vulnerability are essential for true relationships. This entails talking to your pals about your ideas, emotions, and experiences – even when it can be challenging. You develop trust and a deeper degree of closeness with your pals when you are willing to be vulnerable.

In our contemporary environment, developing genuine friendships might be difficult, but the effort is worthwhile. Growing in fraternity will help you to become a better version of yourself and allow you to support others and see God in your fellow friends, thereby creating community around you.

Chapter 39

Memento Mori

'*MEMENTO mori*', which translates from Latin as 'remember you must die', serves as a potent reminder of our own mortality. It is a reminder that life is finite and we only have a limited amount of time on this planet. This lesson is even more important from a Christian viewpoint since it asks us to think about both our present lives and our future lives in heaven.

For millennia past, the concept of '*memento mori*' has been employed in a variety of contexts to assist individuals in focusing on what is actually significant in life. It might be a helpful reminder to put our attention on the things that are really important and to appreciate each and every minute we have in a Christian setting. It is a call to live fully, to love ardently, to forgive easily and to serve others without expecting anything in return.

So how can we remember '*memento mori*' every day? Here are three useful resources that might direct our attention to the value of life and our eternal future:

1. Cultivate gratitude. Gratitude is a great tool for helping us focus on the things in life that are genuinely important. We are reminded of the benefits and gifts that God has given us when we take the time each day to think about what we are grateful for. This routine teaches us to look at the world with thankfulness rather than annoyance or dissatisfaction.

2. Spend time meditating and praying. Meditation and prayer are powerful methods for concentrating on what is genuinely essential. We are reminded of the everlasting truth of life after this world by pausing to be still and think about God's message and presence. Putting things in perspective and keeping in mind how short our time is on earth are both benefits of this exercise.

3. Serve others. Focusing on what is actually essential in life may be done effectively by serving others. Through sharing our time, money and abilities, we are brought back to the truth of our everlasting existence. By engaging in this practice, we may learn to put the needs of others before our own. It also serves as a reminder that God gave us our life to be utilised for His purposes and that we do not truly own them.

Memento mori serves as a potent reminder that life is short and that we should appreciate each and every second. From a Christian perspective, it exhorts us to concentrate on both our future eternal life and our present temporal existence. This reminder may help us live our lives in a way that is true to who we are by practising appreciation, spending time in prayer and meditation and helping others.

Chapter 40

Do not despair!

MILLIONS of people all around the globe look up to St Pope John Paul II because of his message of compassion, hope and perseverance in the face of hardship. He urged people to have confidence, to believe in God and to not be scared of the difficulties and tribulations they could encounter in life through his sermons and teachings.

Here are some words of inspiration from St Pope John Paul II about not being afraid:

> *"Do not be afraid!"*

Let's now conclude with one very important practical tool to take up our cross and live life to the full, so that we make the best use of every moment God gives us upon this earth:

1. Examine your conscience. Examine your conscience before going to sleep, to review if you have lived as God has willed for you in your daily life. If you have

failed along the way, you are able to make a note of it and move in the correct direction tomorrow, and you will become more aware of your day before sleeping. It is important to live every day and every moment, because we are only pilgrims here and there is not enough time for penance and bringing souls to Christ! This will give you the courage not to be afraid of tomorrow.

Conclusion

THE very essence of taking the law of God found in Scripture, Tradition and the Magisterium of the Church is a very difficult and genuine struggle experienced by every single saint throughout history. What makes it even harder to find practical ways to implement this in the life of the Church today is the vast ambiguity in recognising the purpose and mission of the Church. This has unfortunately crippled the clergy and lay faithful to a much lower standard of expectation and execution.

Our focus as a community of *The Catholic Toolbox* is to re-catechise the faithful. This has been a mission in itself, and the people of God (in many cases) are not exposed to taking their faith to the next level and living it spiritually in their actions; liturgically and pastorally. This is the reason why I call this the "second dimension of the Church's crisis". Often, many clergy and lay faithful have recognised the signs and symptoms, yet could not put their finger on the problem and how to address it. This is why this movement of finding practical strategies to target catechetical, pastoral, spiritual and liturgical problems have arisen. How will we have the courage to continue and keep a strong mindset when we may experience discouragement? How are we to assist Holy Mother Church and its members in their varying capacities to implement the faith on a practical level? How do we become like the Word Himself, Jesus Christ, to reach the goal and homeland in mind – heaven for all eternity? What I will touch on will be the collective experience of all faithful Catholics of this millennium.

It is important to understand the climate that you will be facing when you begin to adhere to living your faith more radically in the ordinary world. This is a climate of hostile secularism and simultaneously one of desire for truth by some who have been led astray into the darkness of the world.

I would like to bring your attention to the Easter Vigil liturgy, particularly the entrance of the paschal candle into the darkened church. This is the exact analogy that describes the phenomenon of the change of attitude required. You must be a bearer of the light of Christ, through both learning and living your faith, thereby practically executing the evangelical endeavours in your daily life as you act as an ambassador of the light, and an ambassador of Christ.

Let us go forth and take action with our faith with confidence now that we have equipped ourselves with the tools by practising the 'Art of Practical Catholicism'.

The Ten Commandments:

1. I am the LORD your God. You shall worship the Lord your God and Him only shall you serve.

2. You shall not take the name of the Lord your God in vain.

3. Remember to keep holy the Sabbath day.

4. Honor your father and your mother.

5. You shall not kill.

6. You shall not commit adultery.

7. You shall not steal.

8. You shall not bear false witness against your neighbour.

9. You shall not covet your neighbour's wife.

10. You shall not covet your neighbour's goods.

Prayer to St Michael the Archangel

St. Michael the Archangel, defend us in battle, be our protection against the wickedness and snares of the devil. May God rebuke him we humbly pray; and do thou, O Prince of the Heavenly host, by the power of God, cast into hell Satan and all the evil spirits who prowl about the world seeking the ruin of souls. Amen.

Recommended Reading

Archbishop. M. Sheehan, *Apologetics and Catholic Doctrine* (The Saint Austin Press, London, revised by Father Peter Joseph, 2010).

Deacon Harold Burke-Sivers, *Behold the Man: A Catholic Vision of Male Spirituality* (Ignatius Press, 2015).

Father John Flader, *A Tour of the Catechism - The Creed* (Connor Court Publishing, 2011).

Father John Flader, *Journey into Truth - Instructions in the Catholic Faith* (Connor Court Publishing, 2014).

Father John Flader, *Question Time 1: 150 Questions and Answers on the Catholic Faith* (Connor Court Publishing, 2008).

Father John Flader, *Question Time 2: 150 Questions and Answers on the Catholic Faith* (Connor Court Publishing, 2012).

Father John Flader, *Question Time 3: 150 Questions and Answers on the Catholic Faith* (Connor Court Publishing, 2016).

Father John Flader, *Question Time 4: 150 Questions and Answers on the Catholic Faith* (Connor Court Publishing, 2018).

Father John Flader, *Question Time 5: 150 Questions and Answers on the Catholic Faith* (Connor Court Publishing, 2020).

Karl Keating, *Catholicism and Fundamentalism* (Ignatius Press, 1988).

Ludwig Ott, *Fundamentals of Catholic Dogma* (The Mercier Press, Ltd., 1958).

Scott Hahn (and Benjamin Wiker), *Answering the New Atheism: Dismantling Dawkins's Case Against God* (Emmaus Road Publishing, 2008).

Scott Hahn, *Rome Sweet Home* (co-written with Kimberley Hahn), (Ignatius Press, 1993).

Scott Hahn, *The Lamb's Supper: The Mass as Heaven on Earth* (Doubleday, 1999).

Stephen K. Ray, *Crossing the Tiber* (Ignatius Press, 1997).

About *The Catholic Toolbox*

(Radio show, podcast and consultancy)
www.thecatholictoolboxshow.com

The Catholic Toolbox is a radio show and podcast founded by George Manassa and Akita Manassa, which is broadcast on Voice of Charity Australia (1701AM Sydney), Radio Maria Australia, Cradio Online Radio and many other platforms. It also delivers public talks on various topics of the faith, customised to the needs of our modern world, equipping listeners with practical solutions to live and directly implement their faith in our modern world.

Off-air, it is also a consultancy service, existing to respond to what it calls 'the second dimension of the Church's crisis' — the lack of the practical application of the faith. *The Catholic Toolbox* consultancy has advised parishes, chaplaincies, apostolates and other Catholic organisations in making direct amendments to the enhancement of their catechesis, liturgical life and pastoral outreach — all in keeping up-to-date with the ongoing changes to the social condition and needs of our modern world.

If your parish, chaplaincy, apostolate or organisation requires assistance in enhancing its performance via a private or public consultation, why not consider an independent and autonomous advisory? We believe that external analysis of the problems facing Catholic organisations in effectively carrying out the work of God can be better addressed using an external advisor. This provides both an objective and detailed diagnosis of obstacles to evangelical underperformance, addressed only thereafter by practical solutions and strategies, to achieve effective outcomes, resulting in the salvation of souls.

Partners

The Voice of Charity Australia (1701AM)
www.voc.org.au

Parousia Media
www.parousiamedia.com.au

Radio Maris Australia
www.radiomaria.org.au

EWTN Asia Pacific
www.ewtnasiapacific.com

Cradio
www.cradio.org.au

TV Maria
www.tvmaria.ph

Kreim Media
www.kreimmedia.org.au

Dynamic Deacon
www.deaconharold.com

Bishop Sheen Today
www.bishopsheentoday.com

Notes and Practical Resolutions

Notes and Practical Resolutions

Notes and Practical Resolutions

Notes and Practical Resolutions

Notes and Practical Resolutions

About the Author

George Manassa is author of *The Art of Practical Catholicism* series, and the host and founder of *The Catholic Toolbox* radio show, podcast and consultancy. Co-founded with creative director Akita Manassa, the program has a large audience and provides practical strategies for Catholic individuals and organisations to implement their faith personally and to improve evangelical performance around the world.

George has spent his career working in project management and now as an entrepreneur, trying to bring God to the secular world in the midst of the ordinary circumstances of daily life. His work is targeted to those in the professional, political and social spheres, which seek to bring faith back into the equation, and his goal is to unify the secular and the divine. A firm believer in delivering results, George is trying to fuse these entrepreneurial and business-oriented mindsets to the Church's approach to implement the New Evangelisation effectively, and for all people to take action with their faith practically.

www.ingramcontent.com/pod-product-compliance
Lightning Source LLC
Chambersburg PA
CBHW030305100526
44590CB00012B/532